Dave Lewis

Never Seventeen

A collection of modern haiku

For the great outdoors and the Pan within, or as William Blake
might have said: "If the doors of perception were cleansed
everything would appear to man as it is, infinite."

For Lili

Contents

Introduction

In my first *Haiku* collection (May, 2012) I divided the book up into the four seasons of the year. This was a convenient method of organisation because it suited well the timeline in which I wrote the bulk of the poems, as almost all were penned during one complete year.

So for this second pool of poems, even though I have failed to keep track of the times and places in spectacular fashion, I thought why not stick to using the same system - it seemed to work last time so why change it? The seasonal aspect within many of my haiku makes this a practical solution too.

*

Readers of some of my other poetry books may also have noticed that I can't resist sneaking a few haiku into them as well. *Roadkill* (Jan, 2014) and *Reclaiming The Beat* (Sept, 2017) have several shorter poems interwoven within the pages and even my 2016 cycling travelogue, *Wales Trails*, has a few haiku slotted in too. The latter were frantically tapped into my iPhone whilst halfway up a freezing cold mountain somewhere but that's another story!

My last poetry collection, *Going Off Grid* (April, 2018), has none though. A conscious decision because although I had several I thought would fit quite happily there I also had quite a few more that wouldn't. And so I decided to put together this little volume instead.

It's always been my intention to produce another haiku collection when I felt I had accumulated enough 'modern moments' from my wandering feet and ever more rambling mind, and so here, finally, it is. I also don't doubt there will be another in future years.

*

When I first starting reading and appreciating haiku, I read the Japanese masters Basho, Buson and Issa. Not speaking Japanese these were of course in English translation and by definition approximations rather than definitive. I've since moved on to the more modern, western writers like Kerouac but always return to the old monks because I love their simplistic and uncluttered approach to the world around them.

Recently though I've taken a quick look at some of the so-called *Instagram poets* that can be found online. I couldn't help notice, immediately, two things. Firstly, the majority of these are of questionable quality (that's me being extremely kind), even the ones that have sold over a million copies of a book, and secondly, people seem to love them! Mmm? OK, maybe I'm getting old but I'm a little *confused.com* about all this.

A truly great poet like Issa sweated blood for his art and endured the most tragic life yet some of these modern equivalents have become fabulously rich for churning out absolute gibberish dressed up as teenage angst! The world's just not fair springs to mind.

One of the greatest poems ever written (*IMHO*) has to be Ezra Pound's haiku-like 'In a station of the metro' where he captures his own impression of a series of beautiful people in Paris so perfectly. Now there was a crazy character - he was a fascist, spent thirteen years in a mental hospital but also helped T. S. Eliot with 'The Waste Land', Joyce with 'Ulysses' and Hemingway with his prose so I'm willing to let him off.

Nowadays though someone just has to claim they were hard done by in some small way and they get tons of sympathy and best of all free money. Yep, totally crazy!

*

So what of my own efforts then? As I mention in the introduction to my first collection I have always found the habit of forcing a feeling or the capturing of something special into three short lines and seventeen syllables rather silly. And so just like my first effort I hope that none of these poems fit this rigid and unhelpful pattern. To be honest though I haven't checked.

More experienced and intuitive readers might also think that many of my own so-called haiku are no such thing at all, and that is fine. I'm certainly not going to argue.

Do these brief verses epitomize a single moment though? *Yes, certainly.* Is there always a juxtaposition of two images? *Quite often but not always.* Do I prompt the reader to make an insightful connection between two images? *Hopefully.* Is the appropriate season of the year always alluded to? *Mmm… sometimes.* Do these haiku avoid subjectivity, viewpoint or values? Do they display intellect or wit? *Here, I may have fallen down slightly, lol.*

All I will say though is that what follows is my own version of the numerous fleeting moments, mostly my observations of nature, and quite often human nature, that I have loosely translated via these short impressionist poems.

My intention was not to stick too rigidly to any given set of rules but simply to make you smile and say 'Ah yes, I've felt that too.' I hope I've succeeded, if only a little bit.

3

And finally, what I've also attempted to do with this meagre collection is find some middle ground between the truly great 'nature' writers that I admire so much, like William Carlos Williams, Gary Snyder or Jim Dodge, and many of the prosperous, modern writers that I despise with equal measure. In my own modest way I'd be more than happy to sit somewhere between the two groups.

What follows then is not really a 'haiku' book but a new invention. A subtle, but quite loose collection of events that have befallen yours truly or people I've know. A series of observations and some magical moments that I've been privileged enough to experience.

Dave Lewis, October 2018

Never Seventeen

Spring

ocean art class
driftwood, seaweed, shells
walking from Tenby to Penally

                                    dry stone walls
                          the sutures of the mountain
                        my first ride after the accident

silence after sighs
the river still dripping
from the kingfisher

                            each day more blossom
                                  on the apple tree
                          my teenage daughter smiling

the artist's mother
signing the visitors book again
long day in the shop

pondweed jungle
young frog peeping out
garden quiet

ivy on willow
heron filling the frame
I'm breathing the river right into me

rainbow above the school
I tell my daughter I'll see her home time
then a kiss

trillions of raindrops
are helping the river to move
robin looks on through bamboo

the occasional breeze on my sun-hot back
Ludlow picnic
kisses in the grass

buttoning up your blouse
brushing your long, red hair
- spring again

                    fern growing through the bones
                              of a dead lamb
                                iPhone rings

grey-haired woman
pausing at the grave with the giant toy soldier
- Mother's Day

        I've missed the heat upon my skin like forgotten kisses
                        daffodil sprouts through bracken

birdsong soundtrack to the land
turn the volume up
sun warm upon my face

the brook above the Cwm
is singing a song

                              gorse filled with blue tits
                playing see-saw with the yellow flowers
                      they fly away at the merest breeze

watched by a wretch in A and E
his father's drunkenness
more important than my pain

                        cold water over burnt stones
                    cotton-soft moss on the riverbank
                          my head resting in your lap

cuckoo on the Wye
'I see you!'
alerted by your disguise

pink blossom
reflected in the tired man's eyes
- Cowbridge physic garden

my eyes follow the deer
through long grass waves
- still thinking of you in that dress

tip-toe elegance
then shopping and drinking
back home a different world

the blue skies of April
vanish far too quickly
- then we count the clouds

somewhere between Palestine and Gallipoli
a carrion crow digs for worms
blood-red poppies shine with dew

a trout tastes air
as I watch the maze of midges return
- Taff Trail, Cilfynydd

croaking 'I love you'
over and over
- frog orgy

the rat pauses for a moment
in the working man's house
- austerity bites

dark under the hazel
salmon wait for nuts
- wise moon smiles down

after the funeral wake
I waited for the full moon
- just in case

hen party concertinas out the door
bright-eyed admirers ride the wave of perfume
- the silence at the bar only lasts a second

                              silent in their world
                              I watch the beetles
                                    I am a cloud

a bead of sweat evaporates from my lover's breast
but we'll meet again soon
- storm clouds gather, open window

                    a long train journey is just long enough
                         to complete your fabulous life story
                                             - diesel stinks

harp strings wrinkle
at your touch
Nan comes for tea every Friday

young women in the pub with nothing interesting to say
but still they go on saying
- an empty sky outside

                        knickers riding high above your jeans
            the sum of your parts held within compact perfection
                                - in the forest a sparrow flies

butterfly
on my canoe
let's go with the flow

                                sparrows follow the tractor
                                ploughing the farthest field
                                    farmer's wife looks on

restless young boys loiter
old taxi drivers doze
- neutral nightclub

I block out the sound of a crying child
and focus on the rain
it mixes with the river

                            ravens hover over Pen y Fan
                                walkers come and go
                            ravens hover over Pen y Fan

five swans queuing on the old canal
three cows in a misty field
- heavy traffic oblivious

                            naked without my Labrador
                        glances of accusation at the swings
                Nazi mothers protecting 'Poppy' from paedophile
                                        photographer

double-decker bus
didn't see the low bridge sign
- Ray Bans hide your eyes

'I had ten days in Tenerife, then eight days in hospital,'
said my diabetic acquaintance
- his dog wondering about next week's walk

Roshach's jackdaws
spilled across a blue and white sky
questioning my sanity each Tuesday

darkness coming faster now
wind picking up over Swansea Bay
a hard rain on its way from Syria

dark before dawn
wind blowing rusty beech leaves
crying out loud for love

green mountain stained yellow
two magpies fly over the castle ruins
- I smile and think of tomorrow

tree blossoms above a small plaque
I never knew this dust
- pink snow a week later

body in the shop doorway
as the wind picks up
- crescent moon

crumpled paper
beneath the marble statue
- university library

fern frond birthing
on the busy path
- Mother Nature eh!

boy bounces an orange ball
against the sky blue wall
outside the sun is balanced on the sea

whirl of colour
as the Peruvian girl dances
- slow shutter speed

                              ants crawling
               from under the miner's helmet
                      new builds on the field

light on leaves
lambs glued to the hills
- spring teasing

                                in the square
                            the market grows
                            Marrakech moon

shadows bruise the sundial
in your giant green garden
your hair all teenaged tangles

woollen hedges
green leached fields
the grey rain

                                        chiffchaff from Africa
                                    balanced on pussy willow
                                       - the see-saw of spring

walking uphill
against the gale
your thirteenth birthday

                                              dipper on rock
                                    ripples from drips off trees
                                                      - spring

there's a red mite sprinting across the tablecloth
old dog sighs
teacup steaming

pines in rows
we rest on a fallen branch
traffic noise distant now

                    no app to download
                to feel the green, green grass
            or count the leaves in an oak tree

can a 3D printer
make a kaleidoscope?
A.I. stocks still rising


```
         g o
            l
          d      w        s
        e   s  c    a    p    e
      n    u   a    v    e    a
           n   l    e    a
               m         c
                         e
                       f  u  l
```

alone in her bedsit
sieving sugar
the lumps are left behind

        the homeless girl smiles through broken teeth
         her half-brother sells wraps to school kids
          Victorian clock tower chimes

running rough palms across smooth rock
summer solstice
another ice age coming

        tide lapping moorhen ankles
          warm breeze
        watching your ice cream melt

small heaven
watching sparrows bathe
- the curl at the corner of your mouth

Summer

through forest after forest
through brook and mountain stream
dew drop

our old labrador
always the first
in front of the fire

the Church Inn bed
breasts redden, tower chimes
below us old men drink slowly
- summer afternoon

lustrous pheasants near Kerne Bridge
foggy fields
your sunshine smile through mist

you scratch your scar
nervous
when she drives off

sipping Wye Valley ale amid strange accents
sun showers
on foreign streets

                              even when seen in the morning
               my beautiful princess is still a woman
                                      - birthday in June

sweating redhead
in a tight t-shirt
July the hottest month

                                      an orgy of trees
                                   spurting sunshine
                        the view from our honeymoon bed

frog jumps
from hand to hand
summer move

even a long life is as brief as summer dew
on the hottest day of the year
- August

the smell of tangerines
I imagine your long, soft fingers
sunrise in Sevilla

elephant shadow
painting the ground
plover follows

brave campfire talk of lions
turning in early
Chobe

sparrows return to the leafy garden
dog asleep on the decking
- a month since your hip op

blinded by the stream -
our moments in the sun
shelter under the shade of a tree

my dog's mouth is cold
with mountain stream
- slow summer

digesting the Party's loss
over Sunday dinner
- wishbone snaps

ladybird on hazelnut leaf
sun beating down
- thinking of global warming

you take off your blouse
mist clears
from the river

the orange sun has stopped fighting
water splashes on your feet
as we pack up the beach picnic

she bangs the piano harder
in the summerhouse
- monsoon's here now

deep in the woods
no phone signal
I read footprints

dog walker liking Instagram
summer birdsong, soft skin breeze
...nearly

years after she left
still staring into the distance
- swifts

yellow ball of sun
milky sky
summer's end

               heavy June downpour
                all day and all night
          my dog sleeps soundly next to me

struggling world -
the wind threading its way
through summer raindrops

           the smell of curry from Mr Khan's house
               the policewoman crouches
                behind the castor oil plant

the FTSE up
on the wine bar TV
more 'Spice' victims in the park

buttercups and daisies shake
as the old horse ambles along
- summer field

gulls squawking
blue sky
graduation

my daughter late
I leave love behind
in every field

half-empty glasses
on the decking
August sunset

eyeball to eyeball
with a huge frog
the pond comes to life

radio crackles
outside the summer rain
dry earth

                              midday
                              bubbles
                              under water lilies

old man on the pavement
the bee's final flower
- summer's end

                         brimstone above the brambles
                            pretty girls stuck in cars
                                  Bank holiday

a man's life
over all too quickly
July showers

Saundersfoot sunset
boats bob
seagulls bolt

icy spring water
resting from the walk
mountain in August

Monday
after the funeral
sunshine

sunshine in the street
you cover your eyes with your hand
- fire exit

one last kiss
before he drives back to his wife
rutted farm track

a blackbird sings
our argument comes to an end

blackberry stains
washed in the Taff
girl becomes woman

barefoot on the cracked earth
picking berries and apples
others in offices

the mist upon the river
'What dream? I forget.'

red kite hovering
between postcodes
sofa surfing

you turn the egg timer
swifts outside
the last termites

this town
famous singers, famous bridges
watching jackdaws above the disco

the first bats
in the pale sky
clocks go back soon

loving on a Wednesday morning
Indian summer
woodpecker call

smiling eyes
rain-soaked strawberries
first love?

boys of summer
diving off the harbour wall
Tenby ruins

                    sun through the open window
                         the dog curls up
                  in the chair we still call yours

goldfish sucking air
soon the moon
will replace the sun

                   at the fork in the yellow track
                       'Go that way, dad!'
                            braver now

getting to know myself better
the Kalahari
through the truck window

rugby song chorus louder
last orders rung
– warm bar

evening sky
the bats fly
'I'd best leave.'

starless sky
the terraces by streetlight
despondent

stepping on dry branches
I hardly notice
my creaking joints

peregrine hears
only one pigeon coo
- feathers in the road

'Number 13?'
on the pharmacy chair
worry beads

my shadow killed
by a raincloud
that covers the moon

just a dead fly
in the cardboard bed
lean times for the beggar

my dog comes to say hello
and I can't help but smile
writer's block unblocked

tree swaying
summer breeze
you smell of apples

Autumn

sycamore helicopters
beech leaf carpet
- I'm wandering with the autumn river

September equinox
I give a sigh
you hear it

frost in the park
the old soldier remembers
a colder time

weeds poking through the cracks in the path
money worries
watching the rain

ripples of sand
I swear the sea
knows more than me

kestrel threading contrails
blue autumn morning
'sunshine in my stomach'

the country is turning auburn at the edges
and the sky a distinct cobalt blue
'Make that whisky a large,' she says

the river overflowing
you tell me everything
November flood

autumn leaves falling
the old park runner
rests on an empty bench

both ends burning beneath a blazing sun
but when autumn escapes
sad eyes break

farmer moved out long ago
to make way for community
- needles outside 'the Spar'

                              kettle boiling
                           in the cold flat
              you draw a heart on the window

flowers at the Rocking Stones
rusty oak leaf carpet
October sun

                              burying treasure
                              for leaner times
                                 red squirrel

curry sticks
to the bottom of the pan
I guess no-one will win this argument

Marilyn of the valley bars
they found her dead in the park
- the willow dropping leaves

                    waiting for the doctors to discharge you
                        we see two goldfinches on the bench
                  - the one with the name plate and dates

sunlight through rain
she comes back home
- October morning

                            garden spider weaving
                              an old world map
                              dew becoming sea

we count together
safe in the woodman's hut
- distant thunder

harvest moon
we swap
school memories

                                        church bell rings
                                        leaves all still
                                        waiting for autumn

anxiety class
I'm worried
I'm late

                                        in that brief moment
                                        clouds rush by below
                                        salmon jumping

walking home after the funeral
a single star appears
blue dusk

eating all the pancakes
watching his red car drive away
it's not even Easter

                              St. Catherines church bell
                  every un-Godly hour of every day
                  - the churchyard sparrows restless

your ballet shoes on EBay
in Margam forest
deer tracks

                              the seagull pauses
                        upon Aneurin's statue
                            - Hunt's pen raised

remembering all the old shops in town
but not her grandchildren

BackpacKathmandUncommoNovembeRain

red leaves caught in your spokes
you learnt the hard way
how slippery the road was

answering your questions
in my own time
family grave

the
cross
around my mother's neck
I used
to kiss
when
I was
young

you lose me in Hay
but you always know where I am
- Booths

51

your paw-print fills with rain
as we shelter from the storm
no rush though

                        you always played patience on your own
                                    but now you have to

more Cardiff homeless
as May announces an end to austerity
fog on the Taff

                        little girl hugs her toy lion
                    as the antelope becomes braver
                            - confusion at the zoo

weeping willow
over Roath Park lake
half moon

rust on the roller coaster
October storm surge
- Barry Island

between your dreams and the pillow
lavender

after the rugby scores
and this awful government
'It's an experimental drug.'

infuriated
by a persistent leaf
Bruges mime artist

the ribs of an old fishing boat
crack like cockles
Penclawdd storm

jay in the oak wood
squawking at squirrels
women outnumber men in Wetherspoons

                                    red fox unsettled
                             by the rustling of leaves
                               sun going down slyly

oystercatchers circle
the receding tide
sunset at Penally

                                  a gap in the clouds
                           and life passes before us
                                        - Crib Coch

searching for clues in the sand
after she ran out of the pub
beachcombing

the glow of oranges
in the sun-kissed stalls
- Marrakech

lighthouse surrounded by waves
and modern-day Capas
we're safe in the Pier Hotel

horse hair on barbed wire
you zip up your coat
against the wind

black night
the owl's scream
Halloween

in hiding
behind this argument
another one

my daughter swears she won't get cold
frosty night

      missing coat button
        after the scuffle
      cold wind finds its way in

up to my eyes
in elephants
I'll need a holiday soon

        golden leaf
     hanging by a silken thread
        morning light

kisses
afterwards
so soft

funny how a scent
can crush you after thirty years
- Opium

'Isn't there a way to forget?'
so many great songs
that made me cry

as the plane lands
two geese take off
from the shimmering lake

the dial tone for a brief moment
but then luckily
louder wind outside

waking to the smell
of the same perfume
maple syrup on pancakes

beret shadows on the black marble
etched names shine
in November sun

                              woman puts the photo away
                                 to stare at his name
                                    - red poppies

Post-it note on the floor
of the empty farmhouse
bread, milk, chicken, eggs...

                                    stealing smiles
                                  in a crowded bar
                    I saw you pop in the Pink Shop last week

painting over the pencil marks
6th Form now
seems silly to keep them

Winter

mist clears
but I'm still here with you
- winter cottage

                                        frozen footprints
                                        in the deepest mud
                                        you left last month

the city garden full
of black crows
- knife crime up again

                                        tree uprooted
                                        twisted shape
                                        - your words wound

watching the old woman sing and dance
winter solstice

a flash of young chaffinches
through January mizzle
- hope

deleting my calendar app
winter signing
in the job centre

clouds over Tokyo
driving to
Aokigahara forest

rain on the river
the day you moved out
- windscreen wipers

fog hanging above the river
I never knew why
- divorce

winter sunshine through rusty trees
I'm watching a pair of treecreepers
- in town the church is filling up

                                                        sky blue
                          bare branches in the afternoon sun
                                      - the cancer nurse's uniform

zebra-red flash of song
long morning shadow
- snow in the air

                                                    morning -
                        waves of mist flow down the mountain
                                        this must be New Year

buzzard soars above the crematorium
the hearse empty now
both chapels singing

dead puppies in the river
they escaped the sack
but not this cruel life

laid off workers
sit in the lorry cab
- the rain just won't stop today

the sound of an earthquake
leaf load drops upon snow
shrew shelter

transparent shadow
talking but no-one listening
you walk the icy path at dusk

scattering gravel on dog-walker paths
reclaim the winter mud
- sometimes, just the simplest things...

the winter sun
illuminating the redundancy letters
- plush board room

cold sponge of snow
your hands alive
I'm smiling as I watch you fill with blood

young spaniels chasing perfume around the castle grounds
where pretty maidens used to dance
- snow forecast

a child runs a stick along the railings
magpies refrain
winter dying fast

an elephant born on Christmas Eve
- the star above the penguin pool
brighter

crows pecking
at the ribcage of a lamb
- indifferent wind

old farmer in ploughed field
scratches his brow
mackerel sky

old dog
snoring by the fire
snowing outside

bubble wrap clouds
wind blowing away Jack Frost
- she says sorry

flicking through pages
of old diaries
- can't find me

the textile machines are silent
where dad used to work
- snow blankets the abandoned factory

rainbows turn to snow
a sudden sea breeze
- waterfowl down Cardiff Bay

a pair of ravens
on the mountain top
- we pause to read the plaque

lone pheasant
shivering
February dawn

trying to work out
who he was talking to
- suicide note

her footprints
almost gone
- snow flurry

mist rising above the river
reveals the forest
the things you say when drunk

the smell of bubble and squeak
as I read the December statement
- still snowing outside

empty streets
apart from the raindrops
- Christmas over

worry beads swaying
from the taxi's mirror
cutting city wind

seagull shadow on the sea
the Norwegian Church
full of paintings of ships

homeless girl washing
in the church grounds
- slush

empty shed
dad's tobacco smell
lingers

throwing out dead flowers
as her car leaves the driveway
white roses

Newport wetlands
sunrise
first Shelduck

frog floating
on the moon
clear night

                         she forgets what she was about to say
                          then remembers it wasn't important
                                                   tick tock

you try to catch the falling leaves
from the golden tree
apparently, it's lucky

                                      cactus on the table
                                       roses overgrown
                                       which one first?

confessing all
to her gravestone
it starts snowing

feeling like a tightrope walker
without a net
- Christmas office party

                              her baby struggling to feed
                              she blames Universal Credit
                                          nightjar crying

holding your hand
we cross the icy field
later, we walk back

                    jackdaw balancing on the broken branch
                                above the overturned car
                                            black ice

school snowflakes
my daughter
floating with her friends

ruddock on a postbox
little boy rushes out
to deposit Santa's letter

                              no-one to ask
             the story behind these photographs
                          clearing your house

full moon above the rowan tree
walking home across the mountain
carefree and drunk

                              noisy children
                        'Winter Wonderland'
                     but the stars are silent
                        above the big wheel

the smell of whisky
in the back of the police car
not so loud now

yellow night
fat flakes flurry
the city quiet

                              homeless and pregnant
                    maybe now they'll give you a bed
                as rock doves pick through your cardboard

just the view to worry about now
watching the bulldozers packing up
Llanishen reservoir

                              soaring above Pen y Fan
                    seeing the sun reflect off snow
                                   golden eagle

holding a conch to your ear
a bit pointless
December in Tenby

mead around the druid's stone
Dr Price's ghost smiling
we try

                                        just raven tracks
                                        in the deep snow
                                        farm repossession

morning sunlight on wet grass
hoping love will return
winter walk

                                        crow crawk
                                        the woods hectic
                                in town they're putting up lights

gorse pods coated in ice
hard to get an answer
about the kids

oak leaves glisten
with cold dew
people getting ready for winter too

'Unity' painted red
festive shops bare
bank statement dread

bird chatter around the monument
sirens down in town
guess who got lucky

blue sky ceiling
sun-hot log burner
russet carpet

hard to tell
where the mist ends and the rain begins
ticking terms and conditions

Notes

The following brief notes should not really be needed but are just added for clarity. Some of the poems refer to certain events, history, places of local interest and people close to me and thus some explanation may be necessary to help the reader. They are certainly not inclusive.

Spring

9
A friend has a flat in Penally (west Wales) and we often stroll along south beach towards Tenby and back.

I fell off my mountain bike cycling down Sugar Loaf mountain, Abergavenny and nearly broke my neck so it was important to 'get back on the horse' ☺

Manning the 'Popup Art Exhibition' in Pontypridd town centre I couldn't help but laugh at the mother of one of the contributors who came in every day and pretended to be a random member of the public so she could sign the visitor's book and leave another positive message about her son's work.

11
Not far from my own family's plot, down at Glyntaf cemetery, there is a huge model of a toy soldier. It always makes me think how lucky most of us are.

The 'daffodil' can represent unrequited love.

12
In Welsh the word 'cwm' is a rounded, glaciated valley but the word here refers to a local area where a large, outdoor

swimming pool used to be, hence the capital letter.

Annoyed that drunks and drug addicts get treated first at the local hospital just because they create more fuss.

You rarely see cuckoos (*Cuculus canorus*) but while canoeing down the River Wye I heard the distinctive call only to look up at one above my head on a branch.

13

Cowbridge is a town in the Vale of Glamorgan. It has a rather nice physic garden behind the main street.

The monument on Pontypridd Common has Palestine, Gallipoli and Egypt written on its three sides. The fourth has a tribute to the soldiers that died in the Great War. I walk the dog around this structure most days and watch the carrion crows (*Corvus corone*). Crows are highly intelligent animals and have a similar brain to body size ratio as humans. They also have an excellent memory. In Celtic mythology they are associated with death.

14

The Taff Trail is a 55-mile cycle route in south Wales.

The common frog (*Rana temporaria*) mates in Spring and the adults congregate in ponds, where the males compete for females. The courtship ritual involves noisy croaking by many males. The females are attracted to the males with the loudest and longest calls. There is a bit of a 'free-for-all' at this point.

The word 'austerity' refers to the current Tory government's policy of making massive cuts to public spending. Also, the people that are worse off in the UK are those in work, but on low wages. The self employed, part-time workers, those on zero-hour contracts can't claim benefits yet when you average their yearly income out it is pitiful. I know, I'm one of them!

In Celtic myth salmon are otherworldly animals; their spots being one of the markers of such creatures. The salmon's spots are because salmon eat the hazelnuts of the nine hazels of wisdom, one of which grows at the heads of each of the seven primary rivers of Ireland, one at Connla's Well, and one at the Well of Segais. Salmon are said to bear a spot for each hazelnut they have consumed.

15
I contemplate the water cycle – 'a bead of sweat'

Reading Woody Guthrie's 'Bound for Glory' – 'life story'.

17
Looking around our local Wetherspoons pub, Pontypridd on a Saturday night.

In 1995, after kicking an abusive fan, footballer Eric Cantona famously said to the press: "When seagulls follow the trawler it is because they think sardines will be thrown into the sea." For some reason I couldn't help think about this when watching sparrows following a tractor.

Survival experts will often use the word 'neutral' to refer to the sea or the rainforest. In other words the harsh environment you may find yourself in isn't 'out to kill you' but simply it has no feelings either way.

18

Pen y Fan, is the highest mountain in south Wales and home to numerous birds including ravens.

Feeling anger at the illogical attitudes of some women when faced with male photographers who are often made to feel guilty walking around the park with a camera yet the women who contribute to the planet's demise through over population are hardly ever criticised!

19

Whilst working in Neath I used to listen to the woes of an old man walking his dog.

Swiss psychoanalyst Hermann Rorschach created the inkblot test in 1921 to assess an individual's personality.

Overhearing unemployed locals in a Swansea pub moaning about immigrants taking their jobs.

20

Reading the names and dates of a commemorative plaque in Roath Park, Cardiff.

Watching a homeless man curled up sleeping.

21

Sorting through old photos and slides from a trip to South America.

For 900 years the nightly market in the main square in

Marrakech takes place. It comes out every night and is gone by the morning.

23
A. I. – artificial intelligence

e s c a p e   (canoeing down Tenby)

24
With so much poverty in Wales it seems we're regressing back to Victorian times even faster than most Tories want.

The 'Rocking Stones' on Pontypridd Common were deposited by a glacier after the last ice age.

Summer

27
Church Inn, Ludlow

Kerne Bridge – driving to a portage point, one early morning on the River Wye.

29
Remembering a holiday in Spain (Seville).

Chobe National Park, Botswana, a recent trip to Africa.

My mother got knocked over by two puppies chasing each other on a Labradoodle day I organised. She's 83 years old and broke her femur.

30
Talking about Jeremy Corbyn's election loss after the General Election.

32
Using a little poetic licence I wrote this after an ISIS terrorist was discovered living a mile from my house. The castor oil plant can easily be used to produce ricin. Ricin is a deadly poison, which has often been used as a biochemical weapon by Islamic terrorists. It is highly toxic to humans and animals. Ricin causes cell death by inactivating ribosomes, which are the site of protein synthesis. One milligram is sufficient to kill an adult.

South Wales in the midst of a 'Spice' epidemic. As poverty and homelessness increase so does drug use, criminality and the gap between rich and poor.

36
Saundersfoot, a seaside town in south Wales.

38
'This town' refers to my hometown, Pontypridd, famous for the Old Bridge and singers Tom Jones, Geraint Evans and Stuart Burrows to name just three.

39
From Dylan Thomas's poem 'I see the boys of summer'. Watching the teenagers showing off to the girls in Tenby.

From Robert Frost's poem 'The Road Not Taken'. My daughter getting braver as she gets older and wiser.

From our recent trip to Botswana.

41

Many religions use prayer beads and they have been around
for thousands of years.

Autumn

45

November 11th – 'old soldier'. My great, great uncle used to
say he wasn't afraid in the trenches but he hated the cold.

46

The line 'sunshine in my stomach' is by Peter Gabriel from
the track 'In the cage' from the 1974 album 'The Lamb Lies
Down On Broadway'. I imagine this line was meant to
indicate a good beginning to a drug trip before the
experience goes bad later in the song, but for me it's a line I
always think of when I'm happy. It's such a great line by one
of life's awesome poets!

'Both Ends Burning' is one of my favourite Roxy Music songs.
One I took too literally thirty years ago.

47

Thinking about how developers ruin so many things. The
increase in drug use around new housing developments that
are built on once productive land.

The 'Rocking Stones' are a druidic circle of stones on
Pontypridd Common. Some of which are glacial in origin.
The site has been used by Iolo Morganwg, Dr William Price
and others for bardic rituals. Today, bunches of flowers are
often seen at the site for the stones are opposite Y Bwthyn, a
hospice for the terminally ill.

49

The salmon jumping at the weir on the Taff Trail near Radyr.

The colour blue can have many meanings - faith, freedom, heaven, calmness, intelligence and tranquillity for example. In many cultures blue is significant in religious beliefs, bringing peace and keeping the bad spirits away. In Iran, blue is the colour of mourning.

50

Shrove Tuesday (Pancake Day) is the feast before Ash Wednesday, which is when Lent begins. Christians traditionally gave up something before Easter and went to confession. The colour red can signify love, passion, desire, heat, longing, lust, sexuality, sensitivity, romance…

St Catherines is a large church in Pontypridd with a clock tower.

Margam Park is famous for having herds of various species of deer and they can be spotted during the rut in autumn.

In Queen Street, Cardiff the statue of the founder of the NHS, Aneurin Bevan often has a seagull perched upon it. Former Tory Health Secretary Jeremy Hunt (like all Tories) wants to privatise the NHS.

A good friend who has early onset dementia / Alzheimer's can tell us all the names of all the shops in town, who owned them, who was carrying on with who…

51

The best time for trekking in Nepal (Himalayas) is usually November when the skies are clear, temperatures good and little chance of rain.

Booths bookshop in Hay-on-Wye is the largest second-hand bookshop in the world.

53

'Patience' – the card game played by one player, known as Solitaire in USA. I remember as a child that my mother often played patience when my father was at work or watching TV.

Over the last few years I've noticed more and more homeless in the city of Cardiff. At the same time Tory Prime Minister Theresa May announces at her party conference that austerity (a Tory policy for the last ten years) is to end.

Roath Park lake is in Cardiff.

54

'Barry Island' is a rundown seaside resort, famous now as one of the settings for TV's Gavin and Stacey.

Penclawdd, Gower is famous for it's cockle industry that stretches back to Roman times.

55

The Eurasian jay has been known to bury over 5,000 acorns in a single season.

'Crib Goch' (red ridge in English) is a knife-edged arête in the Snowdonia National Park in Gwynedd.

53

There is a small lighthouse at Porthcawl that is now very popular with photographers, braving the elements, trying to capture the crashing waves. Robert Capa, one of my hero war photographers, who risked (and lost) his life for his art. The Pier Hotel is my favourite pub in the town.

58

'Opium' perfume by Yves Saint Laurent. An ex-girlfriend's favourite. Classical conditioning from university.

59

The 'Pink Shop' is a famous sweet shop in Treforest, south Wales.

Measuring my daughter growing by writing on the wall.

Winter

63

Looking at the crows (harbingers of death) out the back garden and watching the news on TV about London and the recent rise in knife crime under Sidiq Khan's mayorship. London Metropolitan Police statistics show offences in July 2018 totalled 74,487, a 9.2 % increase on the previous year.

64

The Aokigahara forest in Japan is the world's second most popular suicide spot. (The first is the Golden Gate Bridge, San Francisco.) Japanese spiritualists believe that the suicides committed in the forest have permeated Aokigahara's trees, generating paranormal activity and preventing many who enter from escaping the forest's depths. Complicating matters further is the common experience of compasses being rendered useless by the rich deposits of magnetic iron in the area's volcanic soil.

65

At a friend's funeral with a large turnout, I stayed outside in the sun and couldn't help notice a large buzzard gliding above the chimney stack. With my scientist head on I guess the heat from the cremation produces thermals that attracts the birds but still I couldn't help imagine that was 'my friend' flying free of the cancer at last.

66

Cycling along the canal I was nearly sick when I saw puppies floating in the water. It reminded me of Rasputin's final moments.

Watching council workers in a lorry, knowing that austerity cuts had made some of them redundant and wondering why they even bothered to turn up for work.

My dog, Lili, loves digging up anthills or anywhere shrews might be hiding.

68

After reading David Niven's first autobiography again, and then Wilbur Smith's I wondered if I'd ever have cause to write about myself. I dug out some old diaries and was just disappointed.

69

On a ridge near Corn Ddu there is a plaque that remembers a farmer who died in the snow. The raven (*Corvus corax*) is well known as symbol of death and foreboding. Stone Age communities often allowed ravens to consume human flesh by laying out their dead for the birds to pick the bones clean.

The pheasant shooting season runs from the 1st October to the 1st February in Great Britain.

71

'Bubble and squeak' is a traditional British breakfast made from boiled potatoes and cabbage. As a child we often had this meal for tea, as it was a good way to use up leftovers and avoid waste. I never really liked it much but can't help think that more people are cooking this way as austerity bites.

Many Cardiff taxi drivers are Somali (and Muslim) and complaints about overcharging, bad driving, littering, rudeness, failing to finish journeys, refusing to pick up female or disabled passengers and even rape are common. Many people I know won't get into a taxi now with an Asian.

72
The 'Norwegian church' is a landmark at Cardiff Bay. Originally a Lutheran Church, consecrated in 1868. Under the patronage of The Norwegian Seamen's Mission provided home comforts, communication with family and a place of worship for Scandinavian sailors and the Norwegian community in Cardiff for over a hundred years. It's now a popular art's venue.

Although 'white' signifies pure, innocent love, white roses can also represent secrecy. Maybe a secret love affair that you're hiding. White roses may be a way of communicating with an inappropriate lover.

73
Thinking about how angry and frustrated my teenage daughter can get when she's not listened to I thought about getting older and how some (certainly not all) elderly people I know repeat so much trivial conversation. It's as if they are have stopped learning new things, or have no new, interesting information to depart.

74
'Universal Credit' – the new benefit that has left many claimants in poverty. Sometimes known as the 'goat-sucker', legend has it that the nocturnal nightjar (*Caprimulgus europaeus*) sucks the udders of goats causing their milk to dry up. The giving of milk was surrounded by ritual and magic in pastoral communities.

75

The robin (*Erithacus rubecula*) (also known as ruddock) is associated with Christmas because Victorian postmen, who wore red coats, were depicted as robins (on Christmas cards) with a Yuletide letter in their bills. Robins are also considered good luck in the UK.

The rowan tree is thought to protect us from witches and fairies, and is the primary tree of power for ancient Celts. It was called the moon tree because the frosts at the winter solstice would leave stars clustered among the upper branches in what may well have been the forerunner of our Christmas tree tradition.

'Winter Wonderland' – the Christmas fair in Cardiff city centre.

76

The rock dove (*Columba livia*) represents peace and love, but in ancient Mesopotamia it represented fertility. Perhaps because these birds can breed up to six times a year. Wild rock doves, still found in Britain have gradually metamorphosed into our domestic pigeons; they are thought to have been kept as early as 4,500BC, making them a contender, with the red jungle fowl (later the chicken), for the world's earliest domesticated bird. In 2017/18 Cardiff council received 3,987 applications for help with homelessness - an increase of 68% from just two years previous.

Good news for the Reservoir Action Group (a local Cardiff conservation group, formed to fight the development of Lisvane and Llanishen reservoirs, a waterfowl haven just north of the capital city). After years of campaigning Welsh Water bought the site from Western Power Distribution (who wanted to build houses on the site) and are starting a restoration project to safeguard the ducks, geese and other birds, fish and insects that inhabit this SSSI.

The golden eagle (*Aquila chrysaetos*) has been seen as the 'top bird' for at least 5,000 years (there were eagles represented in Mesopotamia in 3,000BC). Many empires and emperors have used the imagery, including the Greeks, the Romans, Charlemagne, Napoleon and Hitler.

77

Dr William Price was a Welsh physician, druid, chartist, vegetarian, conservationist, naturist and all-round crazy character who established the legality of cremation in the UK (1882) when he burned his dead son Iesu Grist (Welsh for Jesus Christ). He married his twenty-one year old bride aged eighty-one in a druidic ceremony at the Rocking Stones, Pontypridd. The place that myself, my family and many others gather, every Christmas Day (approx. 12pm), to raise a glass to the druids, radicalism and madness. Join us.

78

'Unity' is the name of the large statue in Pontypridd that locals call 'the big red thing'. It cost £130,000 and many locals, in one of the most deprived areas in the UK, feel the money could have been better spent creating jobs or helping the poor.

More by Dave Lewis:

Poetry:
Layer Cake © 2009
Urban Birdsong © 2010
Sawing Fallen Logs For Ladybird Houses © 2011
Haiku © 2012
Roadkill © 2013
Reclaiming the Beat © 2016
Going Off Grid © 2018

Novels:
Ctrl-Alt-Delete © 2011
Raising Skinny Elephants © 2013
iCommand © 2015

Edited:
Welsh Poetry Competition Anthology © 2011
Welsh Poetry Competition Anthology II © 2016

Non-Fiction:
Photography Composition © 2014
Land's End to John o' Groats © 2015
Wales Trails © 2016
Happy © 2017
Basic Photoshop © 2017

Websites:
www.david-lewis.co.uk
www.welshpoetry.co.uk
www.publishandprint.co.uk
www.wales-trails.co.uk

Published by
www.publishandprint.co.uk